HLR Press
Southern California

LEGAL NOTICE

Published in The United States of America By Healthy Lifestyle Recipes
www.Healthylifestylerecipes.org

WANT FREE BOOKS?
JUST SAY YES!

New Books Sent To Your Email

For our current readers...if you like receiving free books to add to your collection, then this is for you! This is for promoting our material to our current members so you can review our new books and give us feed back when we launch new books we are publishing! This helps us determine how we can make our books better for you, our audience! Just go to the url below and leave your name and email. We will send you a complimentary book about once a month.

Healthylifestylerecipes.org/Freebook2review

INTRODUCTION

This book will have you making sandwiches like a pro in no time! These recipes are designed to take your level of sandwich making to another level, by "Stepping up your sandwich IQ!". You will notice when using this safe non stick cookware is the only way you should be making meals your kitchen! This book will quickly give you the expertise you need to fully enjoy the benefits of non-stick sandwich cuisine. Today's reader wants quick, short and easy to read paragraphs to make cooking simple but fun, and that's what we have done with this recipe book.

The variety of sections will also have you craving some of the special things that we have for you there. We also have a lot of different sandwiches you may not have been aware of and never thought was possible. But now it's possible in the comfort of your own kitchen! Extraordinary flavored Panini Sandwiches with the taste of bliss, and it's all you'll every need right here at your fingertips!

Show everyone that you are the master in your kitchen. They will think you spent hours to whip up some of these delicious gourmet paninis'.

Now Get to Making those World-Famous Panini Sandwiches... Enjoy!

TABLE OF CONTENTS

Why You Need This Book

You need this book if you want to become a gourmet sandwich maker. Panini presses were created for those who wanted to make a grilled sandwich with other bread – baguette, Ciabatta and Michetta – besides boring white bread. You can stuff your bread with cheese, ham, mortadella, and salami to name a few ingredients. However, you can use the Panini press to do so much more.

Not only is this Panini Press great for making many different types of grilled sandwiches, but it is great at making other dishes in the kitchen –fast and easy for any cook. For instance, you can cook chicken without firing up the grill, grill vegetables, make croutons, and even make dessert cakes – to name a few.

Panini Sandwiches of Any Thickness

Have you ever bought a sandwich maker or Panini press in the past and discovered that you couldn't stuff it to capacity? With this Panini Press you can stuff your sandwich - or other dishes - with as much cheese, meat and veggies as you want.

Most Panini Press' comes stocked with handle lid lock that locks the press in place. This way you can push all of those tasty ingredients inside the sandwich - oozing with cheesy goodness.

We suggest you start stacking and stuffing today!

Nonstick Surface Grids

Nothing sucks worse than making a grilled cheese only to find it stuck to the pan! Did you not put enough oil on the pan? Did you forget to grease the press? A lot of these Panini Press' comes stocked with Nonstick Surface Grids to make sure that your food cooks without sticking.

The Nonstick Surface Grids provides another healthy option for those who are health conscious. Cooking with butter and oils adds more unnecessary calories to your food. The nonstick capacity on the Hamilton Panini Press ensures that you can cook without the butter, without compromising the flavor.

Get the Kids Involved

You have tried different ways to get your kids excited about the kitchen. Well, let the Hamilton Panini Press be another reason. It is safe and easy to use, which is a great incentive to start them off cooking with this great appliance.

From snacks, to sandwiches and even meat itself, bring the kids in for some creative fun. Have them help you start a new weekly tradition – Sandwich Sundays, where everyone can create the sandwich of their dreams and cook it right there in their very kitchen. They will be so excited about their creations that they will want to tell all their friends about it on Monday.

Variety of Sandwich Bread

Bread, there are so many choices to choose from that it can make your head spin. Do you remember when bread just consisted of soft, white bread that was served plain or toasted?
Sometimes it is easy to just go classic, but why not play with all of the possibilities that are now at your fingertips?

When shopping for the right type of bread you can choose from any loaf that is made with barley, buckwheat, corn, gluten, millet, oat, rice, rye, sourdough, whole-wheat, soy or even triticale. The bread aisle contains many options that can not only delight your pallet, but will pair well with the type of ingredients you are going to sandwich in-between the slices – pun intended. Do you ever want to go for an awesome tasting Jewish, Russian or marble rye? A San Francisco Sourdough? And ancient flatbread was well known as focaccia? Or something sweet like Hawaiian?

Whatever you decide, your taste buds are going to thank you for it. Remember, your bread choice is the most important part of the sandwich. So, take it with caution, before you start sandwiching.

Gourmet Panini's Like a Pro

We have all dreamed of being the star in the kitchen. Of making the world's best sandwich. With this Panini Press now you can! You can start with choosing the right bread, and the simplest to tastiest ingredients and spread.

Start with picking the right type of bread for the ingredients you are using. Slather or drizzle the bread with your favorite spread or eat it dry. Pair the meat with the best cheese choice and then top with your vegetables.

Remember, making a sandwich is a science for your taste buds. Whatever you choose will stick in your mind forever as the sandwich that made history. So, start sandwiching.

Wipe-n-Go (Simple Cleaning)

Most Panini Press' nonstick surface makes the appliance easy to clean. No more scrubbing for hours or soaking in the sink. The no stick surface lets you clean it with cloth or Clorox wipe, toss and go. Not only is it easy to cook with, but it is also easy to clean.

This Panini Press will start to become one of the best used appliances in your kitchen. The frame of the Panini Press also lets you store it upright to save space in your cupboards for other kitchen appliances that you might need in the future.

Panini Pro Tips

Making a sandwich is a science. There is a particular meat to cheese ratio that makes the sandwich complete, and if it is not followed then the taste of the dish is completely off.

For instance, using a sandwich spread is one of the essential elements of the sandwich itself. Not only does it add flavor, but it gives the sandwich moisture and a type of creaminess as well. Start experimenting with different types of spreads, to see which one fits well with the type of sandwich you are making. Remember to spread the spread you choose all the way to the edge of the bread to seal against the wetness of the other ingredients you will be adding to the sandwich.

Just like choosing the bread - choosing the toppings on your sandwich is another important choice. Lettuce and tomatoes not only give the sandwich moisture, they also give it a type of crunch and freshness. However, they can add a type of sogginess to the sandwich as well. Instead of tomatoes, you can add roasted peppers to keep the texture and freshness of the tomato. You can use spinach, cabbage or cucumber in place of lettuce as well. Don't be shy. Try something new.

Now Get Panini Making!

A Panini Press is an exciting new appliance that will not only help you create new and exciting gourmet sandwiches, but it will also help you make great dishes without all of the hassle.

Placing chicken slices on the grill helps give it a great flavor, as well as provide texture from the grill marks itself.

Now that you know the press is easy to use, clean and store, why don't you take the time to look at all of these recipes and start Panini making. We promise you will not be disappointed!

BEEF & LAMB PANINI'S

Spicy Horseradish Beef and Cheese Panini

This will hit the spot for any meat lover. The horseradish and jalapeno give this sandwich some nice heat that's balanced perfectly by the cheese

Prep Time: 20 Minutes
Cook Time: 6 Minutes
Servings: 4

INGREDIENTS
1/3 cup mayonnaise
1/4 cup crumbled blue cheese
2 teaspoons prepared horseradish
1/8 teaspoon pepper
1 large sweet onion, thinly sliced
1 tablespoon olive oil
8 slices white bread
8 slices provolone cheese
8 slices deli roast beef
2 tablespoons butter, softened
12 small jalapeno slices

DIRECTIONS

- Combine the mayonnaise, blue cheese, horseradish and pepper in a bowl.
- Sauté the onions in a skillet on medium heat until they become tender.
- Spread the bleu cheese mixture on a single side of each piece of bread.
- Place a layer of cheese, then jalapenos, beef, onions and then a second layer of cheese on half the pieces of bread. Place the other slices of bread on top.
- Butter the top and bottom of the sandwich and cook the Panini on medium heat for 6 minutes, flipping halfway through. The bread should be brown, and the cheese should be melted.

Pesto Beef and Mozzarella Panini

This is filled will lots of classic Italian flavor. The pesto provides an aromatic flavor that pairs well with the creaminess of the mozzarella, and the rich flavor of beef.

Prep Time: 15 Minutes
Cook Time: 5 Minutes
Servings: 4

INGREDIENTS

8 slices Italian bread, 1/2 inch thick
2 tablespoons butter or margarine, softened
1/2 cup basil pesto
1/2 lb. thinly sliced cooked deli roast beef
4 slices (1 oz. each) mozzarella cheese
Marinara sauce, warmed, if desired

DIRECTIONS

- Spread the pesto on one side of each piece of bread. Spread the butter on the other side.
- Split the roast beef between four pieces of bread with the pesto side up and then top with the mozzarella. Place the other piece of bread on the mozzarella with the butter side up.
- Cook the Panini on medium heat for 5 minutes, flipping halfway through. The bread should be brown, and the cheese should be melted

Classic Patty Melt Panini

This is a classic diner favorite. The rye bread, and onions give this sandwich loads of flavor.

Prep Time: 25 Minutes
Cook Time: 4 Minutes
Servings: 4

INGREDIENTS

2 tablespoons unsalted butter
1 large Vidalia or other sweet onion, sliced
1 pound lean ground beef
1 tablespoon Worcestershire sauce
1/2 teaspoon garlic powder
1/2 teaspoon dried oregano
1/4 teaspoon black pepper
8 slices seedless rye
1/4 pound thinly sliced reduced-fat American cheese, about 8 slices
1/4 cup light Thousand Island salad dressing

DIRECTIONS

- Melt the butter in a large skillet on medium heat. Add the onions and cook for about 20 minutes. While the onions are cooking combine the beef, Worcestershire sauce, and the seasoning. Form the beef into patties that are similar in shape to the bread. Place the patties in the skillet with the onions for the last 5 minutes of cooking. Flip the meat once halfway through
- Put a slice of cheese on a piece of bread then a patty, the onions and top with another slice of cheese and top with another piece of bread. Repeat the process with the remaining sandwiches.
- Cook the sandwiches for 4 minutes on medium heat, and make sure to flip halfway through. The bread should be brown, and the cheese should be melted. Serve the sandwiches with a side of the Thousand Island dressing.

Buffalo Patty Melt Panini

These are perfect for game day. The give this sandwich a lovely kick that's balanced perfectly by the cheese

Prep Time: 25 Minutes
Cook Time: 4 Minutes
Servings: 4

INGREDIENTS

2 tablespoons unsalted butter
1 large Vidalia or other sweet onion, sliced
1 pound lean ground beef
1 tablespoon Worcestershire sauce
1/2 teaspoon garlic powder
1/4 teaspoon black pepper
8 slices seedless rye
1/4 pound thinly sliced Swiss cheese, about 8 slices
1/4 cup blue cheese dressing
1 cup mayonnaise
1 cup buffalo hot sauce

DIRECTIONS

- Melt the butter in a large skillet on medium heat. Add the onions and cook for about 20 minutes. While the onions are cooking combine the beef, Worcestershire sauce, and the seasoning. Form the beef into patties that are similar in shape to the bread. Place the patties in the skillet with the onions for the last 5 minutes of cooking. Flip the meat once halfway through.
- Mix the buffalo sauce and mayonnaise in a medium bowl.
- Spread the buffalo sauce mixture on one side of each piece of bread.
- Put a slice of cheese on a piece of bread then a patty, the onions and top with another slice of cheese and top with another piece of bread. Repeat the process with the remaining sandwiches.
- Cook the sandwiches for 4 minutes on medium heat, and make sure to flip halfway through. The bread should be brown, and the cheese should be melted. Serve the sandwiches with a side of the blue cheese dressing.

Corned Beef and Cabbage Panini

This is a perfect way to combine these two favorites. The Muenster makes for a tasty texture contrast to the corned beef and cabbage.

Prep Time: 20 Minutes
Cook Time: 8 Minutes
Servings: 2

INGREDIENTS

1 cup thinly sliced green cabbage
1 Tablespoons. olive oil
¼ teaspoon. table salt
Freshly ground black pepper
1 teaspoon. yellow mustard seeds
2 Tablespoons. unsalted butter, softened
4 1/2-inch-thick slices rye bread with caraway seeds
1 Tablespoons. grainy mustard, more to taste
12 thin slices (6 oz.) corned beef
6 thin slices (3 oz.) Muenster cheese
¼ cup water

DIRECTIONS

- Mix the water, cabbage, olive oil, mustard seeds, salt, and pepper in a saucepan, heat on medium-high heat until water boils. Once boiling lower heat to medium-low heat, cover, allow the mixture to cook for 10 to 15 minutes, stirring every once in a while. Remove the cabbage from the saucepan, and set aside any remaining water in the pan.
- Butter one side of each piece of bread and place mustard on the other side. Top two pieces of bread, mustard side up with corned beef, then cabbage, and finally cheese. Top with the remaining pieces of bread, butter side up.
- Cook the sandwiches for 6 to 8 minutes on medium heat, and make sure to flip halfway through. The bread should be brown, and the cheese should be melted.

Feta Lamb and Babba Ghanoush Panini

This is a great way to use leftover lamb. The beautiful Mediterranean flavors hit the spot, and the grilled pita or flatbread is delicious.

Prep Time: 20 Minutes
Cook Time: 6 Minutes
Servings: 4

INGREDIENTS

1 cup canned grilled eggplant pulp
1 small clove garlic, coarsely chopped
1 tablespoon tahini (sesame paste)
1/2 medium lemon
Salt
Freshly ground black pepper
2 to 3 sprigs flat-leaf parsley, chopped
8 to 12 ounces roasted leg of lamb
4 oval pita breads or flatbreads, cut in half horizontally
1 to 2 tablespoons olive oil
3/4 cup crumbled feta cheese

DIRECTIONS

› Place the eggplant, garlic, 1 teaspoon lemon juice, and tahini in a food processor. Pulse the mixture until it becomes smooth, and then salt and pepper to taste.
› Slice the lamb into bite sized piece. If you use pita bread use a brush to lightly coat both sides with olive oil. If you're using flatbread just coat one side.
› Spread the babba ghanoush spread on one side of the bread. If you're using flatbread make sure it's not the side with olive oil. Put the lamb on top of the babba ghanoush, then top with the feta, and finally sprinkle with the parsley. Top with another piece of pita or flatbread. Make sure the oil side is up if you're using flatbread
› Cook the sandwiches for 4 to 6 minutes on medium heat, and make sure to flip halfway through.

Lamb and Havarti Grilled Cheese Panini

Your lamb leftovers are calling for this easy sandwich. The Havarti adds delicious creamy balance to the lamb and the spinach gives it a nice crunch.

Prep Time: 10 Minutes
Cook Time: 8 Minutes
Servings: 1

INGREDIENTS

2 slices thick hearty bread
1 tablespoon butter, room temperature
1/2 cup Havarti, shredded
1/4 cup leftover lamb, reheated
sliced red onion
handful of spinach
2 tablespoons tzatziki, room temperature

DIRECTIONS

- Spread butter on one side of each piece of bread.
- Place a layer of cheese down, then the lamb, spinach onions, and tzatziki on one piece of bread. Make sure it's not on the buttered side. Then top with the other piece of bread, making sure the buttered side is up.
- Cook the sandwiches 8 minutes on medium heat, and make sure to flip halfway through. The bread should be brown, and the cheese should be melted.

Lamb Panini with Thyme and Roasted Garlic Mayonnaise

The beautiful flavor of the lamb is highlighted in this sandwich. The roasted garlic adds a sweet flavor that pairs well with the thyme and mayonnaise.

Prep Time: 10 Minutes
Cook Time: 55 Minutes
Servings: 4

INGREDIENTS

12 thin slices boneless, roasted leg of lamb
2 heads garlic
1/2 cup mayonnaise
2 tablespoons lemon juice
1 tablespoon fresh thyme leaves
Salt and freshly ground black pepper
4 paper-thin slices sweet onion
Fresh spinach leaves
1 large tomato, thinly sliced
4 soft sandwich rolls
Olive oil

DIRECTIONS

› Preheat your oven to 375F.
› Use a knife to cut off the heard of the garlic cloves. Cut about ¼ inch from the top. The idea is to expose the inside of every garlic clove, and then drizzle with the oil. Bake for 45 to 50 minutes. The garlic should be sweet and soft. Allow the garlic to cool until you can handle it. Then separate the cloves from the bulb. Mash the cloves in a bowl.
› Mix the lemon juice, mayonnaise, and thyme with the mashed garlic until well combined. Allow it to rest for 15 minutes.
› Cut the sandwich rolls in half and spread the garlic mixture on the inside part of both halves of the rolls. Brush the other side of the bread with olive oil. Put a layer of onions on the bottom half of the roll, then tomatoes, spinach, and then lamb, and top with the other half of the roll.

- Cook the sandwiches for 5 minutes on medium heat, and make sure to flip halfway through. The bread should be nicely toasted.

Lamb Panini with Mint and Chili Chutney

The lamb gets kicked up a notch in this sandwich. The mint gives it a fresh flavor, and the caramelized onions gives a sweetness that mixes well with the heat of the chutney.

Prep Time: 20 Minutes
Cook Time: 55 Minutes
Servings: 4

INGREDIENTS

¾ cup Chili Chutney
2 teaspoon fresh mint, finely chopped
1 teaspoon wholegrain mustard
2 tablespoons sour cream or cream cheese
Salt and freshly ground black pepper
4 Panini rolls or olive Ciabatta rolls, cut in half
4-8 slices roast lamb
½ cup caramelized red onion
½ cup feta cheese, crumbled
1½ cup arugula

DIRECTIONS

- Combine the chutney, mint, mustard, sour cream, and pepper. Allow it to rest for 15 minutes
- Spread the chutney mixture on the inside part of both halves of the rolls. Brush the other side of the bread with olive oil. Put a layer of onions on the bottom half of the roll, then lamb, arugula, and then feta, and top with the other half of the roll.
- Cook the sandwiches for 6 minutes on medium heat, and make sure to flip halfway through. The bread should be nicely toasted and the cheese should be melted.

Lamb Panini Burger

The lamb gets a lovely flavor from all the spices. The bread gets nice and crispy thanks to juices and fat released from the lamb as it cooks.

Prep Time: 10 Minutes
Cook Time: 10 Minutes
Servings: 8

INGREDIENTS

2 1/2 pounds ground lamb, preferably shoulder
1 medium onion, very finely chopped
3/4 cup chopped fresh flat-leaf parsley
1 tablespoon ground coriander
3/4 teaspoon ground cumin
1/2 teaspoon ground cinnamon
2 teaspoons kosher salt
1 1/2 teaspoons freshly ground black pepper
1/4 cup olive oil, plus more for grilling
8 thick medium pita breads with pockets

DIRECTIONS

- Combine the lamb, oil, and seasoning using a fork. Allow the meat to rest, covered for an hour.
- Open up the pitas and fill them with the lamb mixture. Use the fill the seal the pita.
- Cook the sandwiches for 10 minutes on medium heat, and make sure to flip halfway through. The bread should be nicely crunchy and the lamb is cooked through.

By Katherine Archer

PORK PANINI'S

Classic Italian Cold Cut Panini

This just like the hoagies you get at an Italian deli. All the flavors meld together so well when they're heated up in and cheese is melted.

Prep Time: 10 Minutes
Cook Time: 6 Minutes
Servings: 2

INGREDIENTS

1 12 inch hoagie rolls or the bread of your choice
1 tablespoon olive oil
2 ounces Italian dressing
4 slices provolone cheese
4 slices mortadella
8 slices genoa salami
8 slices deli pepperoni
4 slices tomatoes
2 pepperoncini peppers, chopped

DIRECTIONS

- Slice the rolls in half and then cut it open.
- Lightly coat the outside of the roll with olive oil using a brush.
- Brush the inside each piece of bread with the dressing. Then top the bottom pieces of bread with cheese. Add the mortadella, salami, tomatoes and pepperoncini's
- Cook the Panini on medium heat for 6 minutes, flipping halfway through. The bread should be brown, and the cheese should be melted.

Prosciutto and Pesto Panini

This a great idea if you want a light dinner especially if you serve it with a salad. The saltiness of the prosciutto is balanced out by the fresh herbal flavor of the pesto.

Prep Time: 10 Minutes
Cook Time: 8 Minutes
Servings: 4

INGREDIENTS

One 10-ounce loaf Ciabatta, halved horizontally and soft interior removed
1/3 cup Pesto
Extra-virgin olive oil
1/3 pound Prosciutto de Parma, thinly sliced
Tapenade (optional)
1/4 pound Fontina cheese, thinly sliced
1/2 cup baby arugula or basil, optional
Coarse salt and fresh ground pepper

DIRECTIONS

- Spread pesto on one of the interior sides and olive oil on the other.
- Put in a layer of prosciutto, then arugula or basil, then cheese. Top it off with a light drizzle of olive oil and a sprinkle of salt and pepper. Top with the other piece of bread.
- Brush the inside each piece of bread with the dressing. Then top the bottom pieces of bread with cheese. Add the mortadella, salami, tomatoes and pepperoncini's
- Cook the Panini on medium-high heat for 8 minutes, flipping halfway through. The bread should be brown, and the cheese should be melted.

Prosciutto and Fig Panini

This is a delicious and simple Italian Panini. The saltiness of the prosciutto is balanced out by the sweetness of the figs, and pepperiness of the arugula.

Prep Time: 10 Minutes
Cook Time: 6 Minutes
Servings: 4

INGREDIENTS

8 (0.9-ounce) slices crusty Chicago-style Italian bread
4 ounces very thinly sliced prosciutto
1 1/4 cups (4 ounces) shredded Fontina cheese
1/2 cup baby arugula leaves
1/4 cup fig preserves
Olive oil

DIRECTIONS

› Lightly coat the one side of each piece of bread with olive oil using a brush.
› Spread the fig preserve on 4 pieces of bread (not on the olive oil side). On the other pieces of bread put a layer of prosciutto, then arugula and top with cheese. Place the fig coated bread on top with the fig side touching the cheese.
› Cook the Panini on medium heat for 6 minutes, flipping halfway through. The bread should be brown, and the cheese should be melted.

By Katherine Archer

Taleggio and Salami Panini with Spicy Fennel Honey

This sandwich is so easy to make but delicious. The lovely flavor of the fennel permeates the spicy honey and adds complexity to the salty flavor of the salami.

Prep Time: 10 Minutes
Cook Time: 10 Minutes
Servings: 6

INGREDIENTS

1/3 cup honey
1 tablespoon fennel seeds
2 teaspoons chili flakes
1/2 loaf focaccia, cut into 4-inch squares
1 pound Taleggio, rind washed, room temperature, thinly sliced
12 slices fennel salami, thinly sliced

DIRECTIONS

- Put the chili, fennel, and honey in a small saucepan and heat on medium heat. Allow the mixture to cook for 3 to 5 minutes.
- Cut the focaccia in half horizontally. Layer the cheese on one piece of bread and layer the salami on top. Top the salami with a nice drizzle of the honey. Put the other piece of bread on top.
- Brush the inside each piece of bread with the dressing. Then top the bottom pieces of bread with cheese. Add the mortadella, salami, tomatoes and pepperoncini's
- Cook the Panini on medium-high heat for 10 minutes, flipping halfway through. The bread should be brown, and the cheese should be melted.
- Top with more honey and serve warm.

Spicy Soppressata Panini with Pesto and Mozzarella

This spicy Italian salami has a great flavor. The mozzarella adds creaminess and the pesto gives a nice herbal flavor.

Prep Time: 15 Minutes
Cook Time: 10 Minutes
Servings: 4

INGREDIENTS

1 Ciabatta loaf, cut into 4 portions, or 4 Ciabatta rolls
1/2 cup basil pesto, purchased or homemade
8 ounces fresh mozzarella cheese, sliced
4 ounces sliced spicy Soppressata salami

DIRECTIONS

- Cut the Ciabatta in half horizontally.
- Spread the pesto on the inside of each piece of bread. Place a layer of salami on the bottom piece of bread and then place the cheese on top. Top with the other piece of bread
- Cook the Panini on medium high heat for 5 to 7 minutes, flipping halfway through. The bread should be brown, and the cheese should be melted.

Muffuletta Panini

This sandwich is a classic from the food capital of New Orleans. The olive salad on top and the 3 different types of pork cold cuts make this sandwich unique.

Prep Time: 10 Minutes
Cook Time: 4 Minutes
Servings: 4

INGREDIENTS

softened butter
8 slices rustic bread or 8 slices sourdough bread
16 slices provolone cheese (thin slices) or 16 slices mozzarella cheese (thin slices)
1/2 cup olive salad, drained or 1/2 cup olive tapenade
6 ounces thinly sliced black forest ham
6 ounces sliced mortadella
4 ounces sliced genoa salami

DIRECTIONS

- Spread butter on both sides of each piece of bread.
- Place 2 pieces of cheese on 4 piece of bread. Then put down a layer of olive salad, ham, mortadella, salami and top with the remaining cheese. Then top with the another piece of bread
- Cook the Panini on medium heat for 4 minutes, flipping halfway through. The bread should be brown, and the cheese should be melted.

Bánh Mì Panini

A Bánh Mì a sandwich is a delicious sandwich from Vietnam. It combines delicious French flavors with some Vietnamese flare thanks to the jalapeno and pickled vegetables.

Prep Time: 10 Minutes
Cook Time: 4 Minutes
Servings: 1

INGREDIENTS

1 petite baguette roll or 7-inch section from a regular baguette
Mayonnaise
Maggi Seasoning sauce or light (regular) soy sauce
Liver pâté, boldly flavored cooked pork, sliced and at room temperature
3 or 4 thin, seeded cucumber strips, preferably English
2 or 3 sprigs cilantro, coarsely chopped
3 or 4 thin slices jalapeno chili
1/4 cup Daikon and Carrot Pickle

DIRECTIONS

- Cut the bread in half lengthwise. Use your fingers to take out some of the soft part of the middle of both pieces of bread.
- Spread the mayonnaise inside both pieces of bread. Lightly coat with the Maggi seasoning sauce, then place the meat on top followed by the cucumbers, cilantro, jalapenos, and then pickles.
- Cook the Panini on medium heat for 4 minutes, flipping halfway through. The bread should be nicely toasted.

Bacon Cheddar and Tomato Panini

This melty Panini will have you drooling. The flavors of bacon, cheddar, and tomato, combine to create a delicious all American flavor.

Prep Time: 15 Minutes
Cook Time: 7 Minutes
Servings: 4

INGREDIENTS

4 Roma tomatoes, halved lengthwise, pulp and seeds removed
olive oil
coarse sea salt
fresh ground black pepper
8 basil leaves, thinly sliced
2 tablespoons unsalted butter, melted
8 slices sourdough bread
8 slices bacon, fully cooked
4 ounces sharp cheddar cheese, thinly sliced

DIRECTIONS

- Preheat a small skillet on high heat.
- Use a brush to coat the cut side of the tomatoes with olive oil and salt and pepper to taste. Put the tomatoes on the skillet with the cut side down. Allow them to cook for 10 to 12 minutes. The tomatoes. Flip the tomatoes about halfway through. The tomatoes should be wrinkly and the tomatoes should be soft to the touch. Check the tomatoes constantly throughout the process so they don't overcook. Once cooked take them out of the skillet and season with basil.
- Spread the butter on one side of each piece of bread. Place 2 pieces of bacon on the unbuttered side of a piece of bread, then 2 tomatoes and a ¼ of the cheese. Then top with the other piece of bread making sure the butter side is on top.
- Cook the Panini on medium heat for 5-7 minutes, flipping halfway through. The bread should be brown, and the cheese should be melted.

Bacon Mozzarella, Zucchini and Tomato Panini

This is a delicious twist on the BLT. You use grilled Zucchini instead of lettuce, and add in creamy mozzarella for a heavenly sandwich.

Prep Time: 10 Minutes
Cook Time: 8 Minutes
Servings: 4

INGREDIENTS

6 slices bacon
1/2 large zucchini, cut lengthwise into 1/4" slices and grilled
3 tbsp. extra-virgin olive oil, divided
kosher salt
Freshly ground black pepper
1 medium yellow tomato, thinly sliced
1 medium red tomato, thinly sliced
1 loaf Ciabatta, halved lengthwise
8 oz. mozzarella, thinly sliced
2 tbsp. Freshly Chopped Basil

DIRECTIONS

- Put the tomatoes on a plate lined with paper towel in order to soak up any excess liquid.
- Use a brush to coat the inside of the bread with olive oil. Put down a layer of zucchini, then bacon, basil, and finally tomatoes. Salt and pepper to taste and top with top piece of bread. Use a brush to coat the top and bottom of sandwich.
- Spread the butter on one side of each piece of bread. Place 2 pieces of bacon on the unbuttered side of a piece of bread, then 2 tomatoes and a ¼ of the cheese. Then top with the other piece of bread making sure the butter side is on top.
- Cook the Panini on medium high heat for 6 to 8 minutes, flipping halfway through. The bread should be brown, and the cheese should be melted.

Sweet and Salty Bacon Cheesy Panini

This will satisfy your sweet and salt craving all at once. The bacon adds some delicious saltiness to the sweetness of the apple butter.

Prep Time: 10 Minutes
Cook Time: 3 Minutes
Servings: 4

INGREDIENTS

8 oz. Brie, thinly sliced
8 pieces thick cut bacon, fully cooked
8 pieces Raisin-walnut bread
½ cup Apple butter
Butter, softened

DIRECTIONS

- Spread the apple butter on one side of each piece of bread. Then add 2 pieces of bacon to apple butter side of one piece of bread and top with ¼ of the cheese. Place another piece of bread on top with the apple butter side of the bread touching the cheese. Spread butter on the other side of both pieces of bread.
- Cook the Panini on medium high heat for 2-3 minutes, flipping halfway through. The bread should be brown when ready.

POULTRY PANINI'S

Bacon Chipotle Chicken Panini

This has everything you need for a heavenly sandwich. The sourdough has a little tartness, the bacon gives it some saltiness, the cheese gives it creaminess, and the chipotle gives it some spice.

Prep Time: 10 Minutes
Cook Time: 5 Minutes
Servings: 1

INGREDIENTS

2 slices sourdough bread
1/4 cup Caesar salad dressing
1 cooked chicken breast, diced
1/2 cup shredded Cheddar cheese
1 tablespoon bacon bits
1 1/2 teaspoons chipotle chili powder, or to taste
2 tablespoons softened butter

DIRECTIONS

- Spread the salad dressing on one side of both pieces of bread. Then top the dressing side of one piece of bread with chicken, then cheese, then bacon, and finally chipotle chili powder. Place the other piece of bread with the dressing side down on top. Butter the other side of both pieces of bread.
- Cook the Panini on medium heat for 5 minutes, flipping halfway through. The bread should be brown, and the cheese should be melted.

Buffalo Chicken Panini

This Panini is an easy way to get your buffalo wings fix. The onions give a little bit of sweetness and the cheese helps to balance out spice from the buffalo sauce.

Prep Time: 30 Minutes
Cook Time: 4 Minutes
Servings: 4

INGREDIENTS

2 cups shredded cooked chicken
1 large sweet onion, sliced
8 slices seedless rye
1/4 pound thinly sliced Swiss cheese, about 8 slices
1/4 cup blue cheese dressing
1 cup mayonnaise
1 cup buffalo hot sauce
2 tablespoons unsalted butter
blue cheese dressing

DIRECTIONS

- Melt the butter in a large skillet on medium heat. Add the onions and cook for about 20 minutes.
- Mix the buffalo sauce and mayonnaise in a medium bowl and toss with the chicken.
- Put a slice of cheese on a piece of bread then the chicken, the onions and top with another slice of cheese and top with another piece of bread. Repeat the process with the remaining sandwiches. Spread the butter on the top and bottom of the sandwich
- Cook the sandwiches for 4 minutes on medium heat, and make sure to flip halfway through. The bread should be brown, and the cheese should be melted. Serve the sandwiches with a side of the blue cheese dressing.

Spinach and Pesto Chicken Panini

This is a delicious light and fresh sandwich. The spinach gives the sandwich a nice crunch, the pesto gives a jolt of flavor and cheese provides some gooey creaminess.

Prep Time: 10 Minutes
Cook Time: 5 Minutes
Servings: 1

INGREDIENTS

1/2 cup mayonnaise
2 tablespoons prepared pesto
1 1/2 cups shredded rotisserie chicken
Kosher salt
Freshly ground pepper
1 1lb. Ciabatta loaf, split lengthwise and cut into 4 pieces
Extra-virgin olive oil, for brushing
1 cup lightly packed baby spinach
8 thin slices of Swiss cheese

DIRECTIONS

› Use a whisk to combine the pesto and mayonnaise. Then mix in the chicken and salt and pepper to taste.
› Use a brush to coat the top and bottom of the bread with olive oil. Put a layer of chicken on the bottom piece of bread, then spinach, and finally cheese. Place the top piece of bread on the cheese.
› Cook the sandwiches for 7 minutes on medium heat, and make sure to flip halfway through. The bread should be brown, and the cheese should be melted.

Dijon and Berry Chicken Panini

This has a beautiful mix of sweet and spicy. The blackberries pair so well with the mustard, and peppery flavor of the arugula.

Prep Time: 16 Minutes
Cook Time: 6 Minutes
Servings: 4

INGREDIENTS

4 Bakery Ciabatta rolls or French hamburger buns
2 tablespoons herb garlic butter, melted
1/3 cup fresh blackberries (about 6 berries)
1 tablespoon honey
1/2 cup stone-ground mustard
3.5 oz. Deli aged white cheddar cheese, shredded
1 medium red onion, coarsely chopped
1 cup fresh baby arugula, coarsely chopped
1 Deli rotisserie chicken, shredded

DIRECTIONS

- Slice the rolls in half horizontally. Mash the berries in a bowl, and mix with the honey and then mix in the mustard. In a separate bowl mix together the chicken, arugula, cheese, and onions.
- Spread butter on the outside of the bread. Spread the berry mixture on the inside of the bread. Put chicken mixture on the inside of the bottom piece of bread, and place the top piece of bread on the chicken.
- Cook the sandwiches for 6 minutes on medium heat, and make sure to flip halfway through. The bread should be brown, and the cheese should be melted.

By Katherine Archer

Chicken Portobello Panini

This is a delicious and simple Panini. The Portobello adds a lovely earthiness to chicken, and the tomatoes add some freshness.

Prep Time: 15 Minutes
Cook Time: 6 Minutes
Servings: 4

INGREDIENTS

1 tablespoon olive oil
1 tablespoon red wine vinegar
1/2 teaspoon Italian Seasoning Mix
1/2 teaspoon salt
1/4 teaspoon coarsely ground black pepper
1 garlic clove, pressed
2 large Portobello mushroom caps
2 slices (1/2 inch thick) large white onion
1 cup (4 ounces) grated Provolone cheese
2 plum tomatoes, sliced
8 slices (3/4 inch thick) Italian bread
1 cup shredded roasted chicken

DIRECTIONS

- Preheat a skillet on medium heat for 5 minutes. Then place the onions and the mushrooms in the skillet. Allow them to cook for about 4 to 6 minutes, making to sure to flip halfway through. Cut the onions in half and the mushrooms into thin slices.
- Brush what's going to be the outside of the bread with olive oil. Top half the pieces of bread with a layer cheese, then, chicken, then mushrooms, then onions, then tomatoes, and a second layer of cheese. Top with another piece of bread making sure the olive oil side is on the outside.
- Cook the sandwiches for 6 minutes on medium heat, and make sure to flip halfway through. The bread should be brown, and the cheese should be melted.

Bruschetta Turkey Panini

This is a great way to get all the flavor of bruschetta in sandwich form. The turkey's light flavor allows, the basil, tomatoes, and mozzarella to shine.

Prep Time: 10 Minutes
Cook Time: 4 Minutes
Servings: 4

INGREDIENTS

8 slices Italian bread
8 fresh basil leaves
8 thinly sliced tomatoes
16 slices of Black Pepper Turkey Breast
4 pieces of mozzarella cheese
4 tablespoons mayonnaise
Olive oil

DIRECTIONS

- Cut the basil into ribbons.
- Place a layer of turkey on a piece of bread, then basil, and then cheese. Spread the mayo on the bottom part of the top piece of bread, and place it on top of the cheese. Brush the top and bottom of the sandwich with olive oil
- Cook the sandwiches for 4 minutes on medium heat, and make sure to flip halfway through. The bread should be brown, and the cheese should be melted.

Southwestern Turkey Panini

This sandwich is packed will all sorts of southwestern flavor. The chipotle mayo gives it a kick, the avocado gives it creaminess, and the Colby jack cheese gives it a depth of flavor.

Prep Time: 15 Minutes
Cook Time: 4 Minutes
Servings: 2

INGREDIENTS

1 medium Avocado peeled and seeded
½ tablespoon Cilantro leaves finely chopped
½ teaspoon Lime juice
Salt to taste
Chipotle mayonnaise (store bought or homemade)
4 slices large Sourdough bread
8 slices Colby Jack Cheese
8 slices Blackened Oven Roasted Turkey Breast
4 slices Tomato

DIRECTIONS

- Mash and mix the avocado, lime and cilantro, and then salt and pepper to taste.
- Spread the chipotle mayonnaise on one side of every piece of bread. On 2 pieces of bread with the mayonnaise side facing up place a layer of cheese, then turkey, then tomato, then avocado mixture, then turkey, and finally cheese again. Top with another piece of bread with the mayonnaise side touching the cheese.
- Cook the sandwiches for 6 minutes on medium heat, and make sure to flip halfway through. The bread should be toasted, and the cheese should be melted.

Smoked Provolone and Turkey Panini

This simple sandwich has a world of flavors in it. The provolone gives it a nice Smokey flavor which, works well with the spiciness of the Dijon, and the creaminess of the mayonnaise.

Prep Time: 5 Minutes
Cook Time: 10 Minutes
Servings: 4

INGREDIENTS

1 round Asiago Cheese Focaccia
3 tablespoons light mayonnaise
2 teaspoons Dijon mustard
5 ounces thinly sliced smoked provolone
8 ounces thinly sliced smoked turkey breast
1 ripe beefsteak tomato, thinly sliced
1 ounce baby spinach leaves
Olive oil

DIRECTIONS

- Cut the bread in half horizontally.
- Spread a layer of mayonnaise and a layer of mustard on the inside of the top piece of bread. Place a layer of turkey on the inside of the bottom piece of bread then, spinach, then tomatoes, and top with cheese. Place the top piece of bread on the cheese with the mayonnaise side down. If necessary cut the sandwiches into wedges in order to fit it in your flip sandwich maker.
- Cook the sandwiches for 6 to 10 minutes on medium heat, and make sure to flip halfway through. The bread should be toasted, and the cheese should be melted. Cut the sandwiches into 4 wedges if you haven't already done so.

The Ultimate Thanksgiving Reuben Panini

This is a great way to use your thanksgiving leftovers. The addition of cranberries to the Russian dressing makes this particular festive along with the substitution of turkey for corned beef.

Prep Time: 15 Minutes
Cook Time: 7 Minutes
Servings: 4

INGREDIENTs
1/3 cup mayonnaise
2 tablespoons cranberry sauce (I used whole berry)
2 teaspoons freshly grated horseradish
1 teaspoon Worcestershire sauce
Kosher salt and black pepper, to taste
2 cups shredded green cabbage or packaged Cole slaw
8 slices rye bread
8 slices Swiss cheese
3/4 lb. carved turkey, thinly sliced
2 tablespoons melted butter

DIRECTIONS

- Mix together the first 4 ingredients using a whisk. Salt and pepper to taste. Combine the mixture with the cabbage until well coated.
- Put a layer of cheese, then turkey, a layer of the slaw, a another layer of turkey, and another layer of cheese on a piece of bread. Top with another piece of bread. Spread the butter on the top and bottom of the sandwich
- Cook the sandwiches for 7 minutes on medium high heat, and make sure to flip halfway through. The bread should be toasted, and the cheese should be melted.

The Thanksgiving Turkey Cuban Panini

This is another recipe that puts your thanksgiving leftovers to good use. This take on the famous Cuban sandwich adds cranberries to the Dijon mayonnaise and adds turkey to the traditional pork.

Prep Time: 15 Minutes
Cook Time: 7 Minutes
Servings: 4

INGREDIENTS

2 tablespoons mayonnaise
2 tablespoons Dijon mustard
2 tablespoons leftover cranberry sauce
Salt and freshly ground black pepper
4 slices good quality Italian bread
4 slices Swiss cheese
2 slices cooked ham
6 slices leftover cooked turkey
8 dill pickle slices
Olive oil

DIRECTIONS

- Mix together the first mayonnaise, cranberry sauce, and Dijon mustard using a whisk. Salt and pepper to taste. Combine the mixture with the cabbage until well coated.
- Spread a layer of the newly made cranberry Dijon sauce on what's going to be the inside of 2 pieces of bread. Put a layer of cheese, then turkey, a layer of the ham, a layer of pickles, and another layer of cheese on the pieces of bread. Top with another piece of bread. Brush the top and bottom of the sandwich with olive oil
- Cook the sandwiches for 6 to 7 minutes on medium high heat, and make sure to flip halfway through. The bread should be toasted, and the cheese should be melted. Once you're ready to serve, slice the sandwiches in half.

By Katherine Archer

VEGETARIAN PANINI'S

Corn and Zucchini Pepper Jack Panini

This Panini is perfect for summer when you can get lots of zucchini and sweet corn. The pepper jack gives this sandwich some heat which is balanced out by the sweetness of the corn. The zucchini gives it a nice crunch

Prep Time: 10 Minutes
Cook Time: 10 Minutes
Servings: 4

INGREDIENTS

1 tablespoon olive oil
1 large clove garlic, minced
1 ear corn, kernels removed
1 small zucchini, quartered lengthwise and sliced
Salt + pepper to taste
8 slices bread
2 tbsp. butter, softened
1 cup shredded pepper jack cheese

DIRECTIONS

- Place the oil in a skillet and heat it on medium high heat. Cook the garlic in the oil for about 15 seconds, until it's fragrant. Mix in the corn and zucchini and cook for around 3 minutes. The zucchini should be soft but not mushy. Remove the mixture from the heat and salt and pepper to taste.
- Place a layer of cheese on 4 pieces of bread, then the vegetable mixture, and then another layer of cheese. Top with the remaining slices of bread. Butter both the top and bottom of the sandwich.
- Cook the Panini on high heat for 5 to 7 minutes, flipping halfway through. The bread should be brown, and the cheese should be melted.

Lemony Delicious Summer Vegetable Panini

This Panini has all the bounty of summer, and a nice light lemony flavor. It's the perfect light summer lunch filled with vegetables and creamy ricotta cheese.

Prep Time: 15 Minutes
Cook Time: 4 Minutes
Servings: 4

INGREDIENTS

1 tablespoons olive oil
1 small onion, sliced
1 medium yellow squash, thinly sliced
1 medium zucchini, thinly sliced
1 red bell pepper, sliced
2 teaspoons + lemon zest
¼ teaspoon salt
4 Ciabatta rolls or 4 pieces of focaccia
1/8 teaspoon ground black pepper
1 cup part-skim ricotta cheese
2 teaspoons lemon zest
1 ½ teaspoons lemon juice
1/8 teaspoon salt
1/8 teaspoon ground black pepper

DIRECTIONS

- Place the oil in a skillet and heat it on medium high heat. Cook the onions in the oil for about 3 to 4 seconds, until they start to soften. Mix in the squash, peppers and zucchini and cook for another 5 to 7 minutes. Mix in the first 2 teaspoons of lemon zest and 1/8 teaspoon of pepper and the ¼ teaspoon of salt. Remove the mixture from the heat and set aside in a bowl.
- Mix the last 5 ingredients in a bowl.
- Slice the rolls in half horizontally and place a layer of the ricotta mixture on the inside of each piece of bread.
- Place the vegetable mixture on the bottom pieces of bread. Pot the top pieces of bread on the vegetables, making sure the ricotta side is touching the vegetables.

- Cook the Panini on medium high heat for 3 to 4 minutes, flipping halfway through. The bread should be brown, and the cheese should be melted.

Provolone Baby Mushroom and Caramelized Onion Panini

This Panini is the closest thing you're going to get to French onion soup in sandwich form. The caramelized onions are just like the onions found in French onion soup, and your bread mimics the delicious top of the soup. The mushrooms sop up all the delicious caramelized onion flavor and add a light earthiness.

Prep Time: 40 Minutes
Cook Time: 4 Minutes
Servings: 5

INGREDIENTS

2 tablespoons unsalted butter
2 tablespoons olive oil
1 and 1/2 large onions (or 2 medium) sliced into 1/4 inch thick slices
1 tablespoon sugar
1/4 teaspoon thyme
2 tablespoons minced garlic (I used 1 and 1/2)
1 teaspoon Worcestershire sauce
8 oz. fresh baby Bella mushrooms, sliced into 1/4 inch thick slices
1/2 teaspoon black pepper
salt to taste
1/4 - 1/2 teaspoon red pepper flakes (or more to taste)
1 teaspoon flour
1/4 cup mushroom broth (or beef broth)
2 tablespoons minced parsley
5 - 1 oz. slices provolone cheese, cut in half
10 slices of fresh French bread
Olive oil

DIRECTIONS

› Heat a big skillet on medium heat, making sure it's hot before adding any ingredients. Put in the olive oil and butter, and allow the butter to melt. Then put in the onions and allow them to cook for 5 minutes. Mix in the sugar and cook for an additional 15 minutes. Mix in the Worchester sauce, garlic, and thyme, and allow the mixture to cook for 2 more minutes before mixing in the mushrooms. Cook for 10 minutes before mixing in the red and black pepper along with the flour. Slowly mix in the broth 1 tablespoon at a time, waiting until it's been absorbed before adding another. After you've added all of the broth and it's been absorbed, remove it from the heat and mix in the parsley.

- Place a layer of cheese on 5 pieces of bread, then the vegetable mixture, and then another layer of cheese. Top with the remaining slices of bread. Brush the olive oil on both the top and bottom of the sandwiches.
- Cook the Panini on medium high heat for 3 to 4 minutes, flipping halfway through. The bread should be toasted, and the cheese should be melted.

Hummus and Vegetable Panini

This Panini is incredibly easy to make, and so light and fresh. It's packed with wholesome vegetable, and delicious hummus.

Prep Time: 10 Minutes
Cook Time: 5 Minutes
Servings: 4

INGREDIENTS

1 tablespoons olive oil
1 small onion, sliced
1 medium zucchini, thinly sliced
1 medium cucumber, thinly sliced
1 red bell pepper, sliced
8 slices whole grain bread
4 tablespoon homemade or store bought hummus of your choice
fresh spinach leaves
1 cup matchstick carrots
slice of provolone cheese

DIRECTIONS

- Spread the hummus on 1 side of 4 pieces of bread. Layer the vegetables starting with the zucchini, then, cucumber, then spinach then red bell pepper, then carrots. Top the vegetables with a slice of cheese and place another piece of bread on the cheese. Brush the top and bottom of the sandwich with the olive oil
- Cook the Panini on medium heat for 4 to 5 minutes, flipping halfway through. The bread should be brown, and the cheese should be melted.

Shaved Asparagus and Balsamic Cherries with Pistachios Panini

This Panini is a strange mix of flavor combinations. I'm sure you would never think to put cherries and asparagus together but they work.

Prep Time: 15 Minutes
Cook Time: 6 Minutes
Servings: 4

INGREDIENTS

1 to 1 and 1/2 cups pitted, chopped Bing cherries
zest from 2 lemons
3 to 4 tbsp. balsamic vinegar
roughly 1/2 bunch of thick-stalk asparagus, shaved with a mandolin or vegetable peeler
2 tbsp. fresh mint, thinly sliced
2 tbsp. fresh basil, thinly sliced
2 tbsp. pistachio oil
1 multigrain baguette, cut in half, and split open
ricotta
fresh mozzarella
salt and freshly-cracked pepper
1/2 tbsp. butter, softened

DIRECTIONS

- Mix the cherries, balsamic vinegar, and lemon zest. Then salt and pepper to taste.
- Mix the asparagus mint, pistachio oil, and basil in a different bowl.
- Cut the mozzarella into slices that are 1/3 of an inch thick. Place them on the inside part of the pieces of bread and place the cherry mixture on top of it. Then place the asparagus mixture on top of that
- Use a knife top spread the ricotta on the inside of the top pieces of bread, and place it on the asparagus mixture.
- Cook the Panini on medium heat for 5 to 6 minutes, flipping halfway through. The bread should be brown, and the cheese should be melted.
- Cut the sandwiches in half before serving.

Avocado and Mixed Vegetable Panini

This Panini is so delicious and creamy thanks to the cheese and avocado. The sautéed vegetable is packed with flavor and all sorts of good vitamins and minerals.

Prep Time: 15 Minutes
Cook Time: 20 Minutes
Servings: 4

INGREDIENTS

1 1/2 tablespoons butter or olive oil
1 minced shallot (onion or garlic works too)
8 ounces sliced baby Portobello mushrooms
1 cup cherry or grape tomatoes
2 cups chopped kale, stems removed
salt to taste
2 avocados
8 pieces thick, sturdy wheat bread
White cheese like Provolone or Mozzarella
Olive oil

DIRECTIONS

- Put the butter in a big skillet and allow it to melt on medium heat. Put in the shallots and cook until they become translucent. Mix in the mushrooms, and cook until they start to brown. Then mix in the kale and tomatoes, and cook until the kale wilts, and the tomatoes are cooked through.
- Mash the avocados using a fork. Spread the avocado on what's going to be the inside of each piece of bread. Then place a layer of cheese on half of the pieces of bread, then a layer of veggies, and finally another layer of cheese. Top with another piece of bread. Brush the top and bottom of the sandwich with olive oil
- Cook the Panini on medium heat for 4 to 5 minutes, flipping halfway through. The bread should be brown, and the cheese should be melted.

Thai Peanut Peach Panini with Basil

This makes a delicious and unexpected dessert. The sweetness of the peaches is well paired by the creaminess of the peanut sauce, and the aromatic flavor of the basil.

Prep Time: 10 Minutes
Cook Time: 8 Minutes
Servings: 1

INGREDIENTS

2 tbsp. creamy natural peanut butter
1 tbsp. agave or maple syrup
1/2 tbsp. soy sauce or tamari
1/2 tbsp. lime juice
2 slices good sandwich bread
1 small or 1/2 large peach sliced thin
2 tbsp. fresh basil leaves
1-2 tsp. olive oil
Butter, softened

DIRECTIONS

- Mix together the first 4 ingredients using a whisk. If the sauce is too thick you can thin it out with a small amount of water. The sauce will natural thin when it's grilled.
- Spread a large amount of the peanut sauce on what's going to be the inside pieces of bread. Layer the peaches and basil on the peanut sauce side of one of the pieces of bread, and then top with the other. Spread the butter on the top and bottom of the sandwich
- Cook the Panini on medium heat for 6 to 8 minutes, flipping halfway through. The bread should be brown, and the cheese should be melted.

By Katherine Archer

Vegan Pepper Jack Roasted Pepper Panini

This spicy sandwich will hit the spot for any vegan. The peppers provide a world of flavor, the vegan cheese adds creaminess, and the Harissa adds some lovely heat.

Prep Time: 10 Minutes
Cook Time: 4 Minutes
Servings: 1

INGREDIENTS

2 slices bread (sourdough used)
2 tsp. vegan buttery spread
5 thin slices of tomato
1/4 cup (handful) of fresh basil leaves
1/4 - 1/3 cup vegan pepper jack cheese shreds such as Daiya
2-3 thin slices roasted red or yellow pepper
1/2 cup baby spinach
pinches of black pepper
jacklespoon Harissa

DIRECTIONS

- Spread what's going to be the outside of each piece of bread with the vegan buttery spread. Spread the Harissas on what's going to be the inside of each piece of bread.
- Place the tomatoes on one of the pieces of bread, then the spinach, then the basil, then the peppers, and top with the vegan cheese. Place the other piece of bread on top with the Harissa touching the cheese.
- Cook the Panini on medium heat for 2 to 4 minutes, flipping halfway through. The bread should be brown, and the cheese should be melted.

Peach Caprese Panini

This is like having a delightful caprese salad with a sweet twist. The peach gives it a delightful sweetness that's balanced by the creamy mozzarella, the aromatic flavor of the basil, and the tartness of the balsamic vinegar. Try using burrata instead of mozzarella for even more creaminess

Prep Time: 10 Minutes
Cook Time: 4 Minutes
Servings: 1

INGREDIENTS

1 French deli roll, split
1 ½ teaspoon balsamic vinegar
2 slices mozzarella cheese
1 small heirloom tomato, sliced
4 fresh basil leaves
olive oil
1 small peach, sliced

DIRECTIONS

› Sprinkle the balsamic vinegar on the inside of both pieces of bread. Brush the outside of both pieces of bread with olive oil
› Place one of the mozzarella slices on the bottom piece of bread, then the peaches, then the tomatoes, and top with the other piece of cheese. Place the other piece of bread on top of the cheese.
› Cook the Panini on medium heat for 3 to 4 minutes, flipping halfway through. The bread should be toasted, and the cheese should be melted.

By Katherine Archer

Ratatouille Panini

This is a take on the classic French dish. It makes for a delicious, healthy vegetarian sandwich that's perfect for lunch. The roasted red pepper sauce gives it a lot of flavor.

Prep Time: 30 Minutes
Cook Time: 16 Minutes
Servings: 1

INGREDIENTS

1 red bell pepper, sliced
1 tomato, chopped
1 clove garlic, minced
1 teaspoon dried oregano, or to taste
salt and ground black pepper to taste
1 eggplant, sliced
1 zucchini, sliced
1 tomato, sliced
1 red onion, sliced
4 teaspoons olive oil
4 slices sourdough bread
4 slices mozzarella cheese

DIRECTIONS

- Warm a skillet on high heat, and place the red bell pepper in it for around 5 minutes. The pepper should be soft when it's ready. Place the red pepper, chopped tomato, garlic in a blender or food processor. Blend or process until a smooth sauce is formed. Add salt, pepper, and oregano to taste.
- Grill the remaining vegetable on a grille or the same skillet for about 6 minutes flipping halfway through. The vegetables will be soft when ready.
- Brush what's going to be the outside of the bread slices with olive oil. Spread the sauce on what's going to be the inside of the bread. Layer a piece of piece of cheese on 2 of the pieces of bread, then the vegetable mixture, then another piece of cheese. Top with another piece of bread with the sauce side touching the cheese.
- Cook the Panini on medium heat for 4 to 5 minutes, flipping halfway through. The bread should be toasted, and the cheese should be melted.

BREAKFAST PANINI'S

Bacon Egg and Sausage Breakfast Panini

This Panini is perfect for all meat lovers. It's packed with so much flavor thanks to the meat, cheese, bell pepper, and pesto. It's so good you might want 2!

Prep Time: 20 Minutes
Cook Time: 6 Minutes
Servings: 2

INGREDIENTS

2 pita breads
1/2cup pesto
2 eggs
1 cup shredded sharp cheddar cheese
1 cup shredded Monterey Jack cheese
1 cup shredded mozzarella cheese
1 pork sausage patty, cooked
2 strips bacon, cooked
1/3 cup roasted red pepper
1-2 tablespoons butter, melted
2 scallions, chopped

DIRECTIONS

› Use a whisk to beat the egg with a pinch of salt and pepper. Place the butter in a skillet and melt it on medium heat. Use a spoon to stir the eggs and push them across the pan. Cook until the eggs set, about 1 to 2 minutes.

› Chop the sausage into small pieces. Spread the pesto on half of both pieces of pita. Top the pitas with half the cheese, then eggs, bacon, sausage, bell pepper, the remaining, cheese and then top with the scallions. Fold the other side of the pita on top of the filling, and spread the butter on the outside of the pitas.

› Cook the Panini on medium heat for 4 to 6 minutes, flipping halfway through. The bread should be brown, and the cheese should be melted.

French Toast and Grilled Banana Panini

This Panini is a banana lover's dream. The perfectly caramelized bananas are only enhanced by the wonderful flavor of the French toast, creating a sandwich everyone in your family will love!

Prep Time: 20 Minutes
Cook Time: 6 Minutes
Servings: 4

INGREDIENTS

6 large eggs
1 cup whole milk
1/2 cup heavy cream
1/4 cup fresh orange juice (from about 1 medium orange)
2 tablespoons vanilla extract
2 tablespoons cognac (optional)
2 tablespoons granulated sugar
1/2 teaspoon ground cinnamon
Pinch of freshly grated nutmeg
Salt
8 slices Texas toast or other thick white bread
3 large ripe bananas
2 tablespoons unsalted butter, melted
Confectioners' sugar, for garnish
Pure maple syrup, for garnish

DIRECTIONS

- Use a whisk to combine the eggs, milk, cream, orange juice, cognac, sugar, cinnamon, and vanilla. Put the bread in a couple of shallow baking dishes and cover with the mixture you just created. Allow the bread to rest in the mixture for 10 minutes
- While the bread is resting preheat a skillet on medium heat. Then coat the bananas with melted butter and cook them in the skillet until are nice and brown all over, about 3 minutes. They should be releasing their juices. When bananas have cooled down a little chop them into chunks.

- Preheat your flip sandwich maker on medium high heat. While that's preheating place the bananas on half the pieces of bread and top with the other pieces of bread.
- Cook the Panini for 6 to 7 minutes in your preheated flap sandwiched maker, flipping halfway through.
- Top with confectioners' sugar and maple syrup

Chocolate Hazelnut French Toast Panini

This Panini has a beautiful flavor profile. The richness of the chocolate hazelnut spread provides some richness to the sweetness of the French toast, and the hazelnuts provide a perfect crunch in contrast to the soft inside of the French toast!

Prep Time: 20 Minutes
Cook Time: 6 Minutes
Servings: 4

INGREDIENTS

6 large eggs
1 cup whole milk
1/2 cup heavy cream
1/4 cup fresh orange juice (from about 1 medium orange)
2 tablespoons vanilla extract
2 tablespoons cognac (optional)
2 tablespoons granulated sugar
1/2 teaspoon ground cinnamon
Pinch of freshly grated nutmeg
Salt
8 slices Texas toast or other thick white bread
½ cup hazelnut spread with cocoa
¼ cup chopped hazelnuts, toasted
Confectioners' sugar, for garnish
Pure maple syrup, for garnish

DIRECTIONS

- Spread the hazelnut spread on 4 of the pieces of bread and then place the hazelnuts on top. Top with the pieces of bread.
- Use a whisk to combine the eggs, milk, cream, orange juice, cognac, sugar, cinnamon, and vanilla. Put the sandwiches in a shallow baking dishes and cover with the mixture you just created. Allow the sandwiches to rest in the mixture for 10 minutes
- Preheat your flip sandwich maker on medium high heat.

- Cook the Panini for 6 to 7 minutes in your preheated flap sandwiched maker, flipping halfway through.
- Top with confectioners' sugar and maple syrup

French Toast and Strawberries in Cream Panini

This Panini will a huge hit with your kids. The cream cheese mixes perfectly with the strawberries as a delicious surprise in the middle of two delicious pieces of French toast!

Prep Time: 20 Minutes
Cook Time: 6 Minutes
Servings: 4

INGREDIENTS

6 large eggs
1 cup whole milk
1/2 cup heavy cream
1/4 cup fresh orange juice (from about 1 medium orange)
2 tablespoons vanilla extract
2 tablespoons cognac (optional)
2 tablespoons granulated sugar
1/2 teaspoon ground cinnamon
Pinch of freshly grated nutmeg
Salt
8 slices Texas toast or other thick white bread
1/2 cup cream cheese
1/2 cup of strawberries, sliced thinly + 1/4 cup strawberries cut into small pieces
Confectioners' sugar, for garnish
Pure maple syrup, for garnish

DIRECTIONS

- Spread the cream cheese on what's going to be the inside of the pieces of bread and then place the strawberries on top of 4 of them. Top with the remaining pieces of bread.
- Use a whisk to combine the eggs, milk, cream, orange juice, cognac, sugar, cinnamon, and vanilla. Put the sandwiches in a shallow baking dishes and cover with the mixture you just created. Allow the sandwiches to rest in the mixture for 10 minutes.
- Preheat your flip sandwich maker on medium high heat.

- Cook the Panini for 6 to 7 minutes in your preheated flap sandwiched maker, flipping halfway through.
- Top with confectioners' sugar and maple syrup

Mixed Berry French Toast Panini

This Panini has all the berry flavor you can handle. The creaminess of the cream cheese enhances the flavors of the raspberries and blackberries. Use frozen berries if you can't find fresh ones, but make sure to thaw them out first.

Prep Time: 20 Minutes
Cook Time: 6 Minutes
Servings: 4

INGREDIENTS

6 large eggs
1 cup whole milk
1/2 cup heavy cream
1/4 cup fresh orange juice (from about 1 medium orange)
2 tablespoons vanilla extract
2 tablespoons cognac (optional)
2 tablespoons granulated sugar
1/2 teaspoon ground cinnamon
Pinch of freshly grated nutmeg
Salt
8 slices Texas toast or other thick white bread
1 cup blackberries
1 cup raspberries
Confectioners' sugar, for garnish
Pure maple syrup, for garnish

DIRECTIONS

- Spread the cream cheese on what's going to be the inside of the pieces of bread and then place the strawberries on top of 4 of them. Top with the remaining pieces of bread.
- Use a whisk to combine the eggs, milk, cream, orange juice, cognac, sugar, cinnamon, and vanilla. Put the sandwiches in a shallow baking dishes and cover with the mixture you just created. Allow sandwiches to rest in the mixture for 10 minutes.
- Preheat your flip sandwich maker on medium high heat.
- Cook the Panini for 6 to 7 minutes in your preheated flap sandwiched maker, flipping halfway through.
- Top with confectioners' sugar and maple syrup.

Spicy Chocolate Hazelnut Bacon French Toast Panini

This Panini is has so many delicious layers of flavor. You get delicious nuttiness from the chocolate hazelnut spread, heat from the cayenne, and saltiness from the bacon.

Prep Time: 20 Minutes
Cook Time: 6 Minutes
Servings: 4

INGREDIENTS

6 large eggs
1 cup whole milk
1/2 cup heavy cream
1/4 cup fresh orange juice (from about 1 medium orange)
2 tablespoons vanilla extract
2 tablespoons cognac (optional)
2 tablespoons granulated sugar
1/2 teaspoon ground cinnamon
Pinch of freshly grated nutmeg
Salt
Cayenne Pepper
8 strips of bacon, cooked
8 slices Texas toast or other thick white bread
½ cup hazelnut spread with cocoa
¼ cup chopped hazelnuts, toasted
Confectioners' sugar, for garnish
Pure maple syrup, for garnish

DIRECTIONS

› Spread the hazelnut spread on 4 of the pieces of bread and then place the bacon on top. Add cayenne pepper to taste. Top with the pieces of bread.
› Use a whisk to combine the eggs, milk, cream, orange juice, cognac, sugar, cinnamon, and vanilla. Put the sandwiches in a shallow baking dishes and cover with the mixture you just created. Allow the sandwiches to rest in the mixture for 10 minutes

- Preheat your flip sandwich maker on medium high heat.
- Cook the Panini for 6 to 7 minutes in your preheated flap sandwiched maker, flipping halfway through.
- Top with confectioners' sugar and maple syrup

Prosciutto and Egg Bagel Panini

This Panini is great for breakfast sandwich and bagel lovers. The prosciutto adds a nice saltiness to the cheese, and the rich flavor of the eggs. Use your favorite bagel to make it special!

Prep Time: 10 Minutes
Cook Time: 3 Minutes
Servings: 2

INGREDIENTS

2 eggs
2 everything bagels (or any favorite bagel)
2 tablespoons mayonnaise
2 slices American cheese
4 slices prosciutto
2 handfuls baby arugula
Kosher salt
Ground black pepper
Olive oil
2 teaspoon butter

DIRECTIONS

- Use a whisk to beat the egg with a pinch of salt and pepper. Place the butter in a skillet and melt it on medium heat. Use a spoon to stir the eggs and push them across the pan. Cook until the eggs set, about 1 to 20 minutes.
- Cut the bagels in half horizontally. Spread the mayonnaise on the inside of the bagel. Layer the eggs, on the inside of 2 of the bagel halves, then the cheese, then the arugula, then the prosciutto. Top with the remaining pieces of bagel. Brush the top and bottom of the sandwiches with olive oil.
- Cook the Panini on medium heat for 2 to 3 minutes, flipping halfway through. The bagels should be toasted, and the cheese should be melted.

Harissa Avocado Sausage and Egg Breakfast Panini

This Panini is filled with Mediterranean flavor. The Harissa and pepper jack give this some heat, the arugula provides a peppery flavor, and the Merguez has a beautiful spiced flavor.

Prep Time: 15 Minutes
Cook Time: 6 Minutes
Servings: 2

INGREDIENTS

4 pieces of sourdough or crusty bread
¼ cup Harissa
2 eggs
½ avocado, sliced into pieces
1 cup pepper jack cheese
A handful of arugula
2 Merguez sausages, cooked
Olive oil
2 teaspoon butter

DIRECTIONS

- Use a whisk to beat the egg with a pinch of salt and pepper. Place the butter in a skillet and melt it on medium heat. Use a spoon to stir the eggs and push them across the pan. Cook until the eggs set, about 1 to 2 minutes.
- Chop the sausage into small pieces or butterfly them. Spread the Harissa on what's going to be the inside of two pieces of bread. Put a layer of egg on the Harissa side of the 2 pieces of bread, then the sausage, then the arugula, then avocado and top with the cheese. Then place the other two pieces of bread on top of the cheese. Brush the top and bottom of the sandwiches with olive oil.
- Cook the Panini on medium heat for 4 to 6 minutes, flipping halfway through. The bread should be toasted, and the cheese should be melted.

Pancetta Cherry Tomato and Egg English Muffin Panini

This Panini features a variety of flavors. Pancetta is like an Italian form of bacon, the cherry tomatoes give it sweetness, and the mozzarella gives it creaminess.

Prep Time: 15 Minutes
Cook Time: 6 Minutes
Servings: 1

INGREDIENTS

1 English muffin
1 egg
5 cherry tomatoes
Fresh basil, chopped
2 slices of mozzarella
Olive oil
1 teaspoon butter
4 thin slices of pancetta, cooked

DIRECTIONS

- Use a whisk to beat the egg with a pinch of salt and pepper. Place the butter in a skillet and melt it on medium heat. Use a spoon to stir the eggs and push them across the pan. Cook until the eggs set, about 1 to 2 minutes.
- Put a layer of avocado on the Harissa side of the 2 pieces of bread, then the sausage, then the arugula, and top with the cheese. Then place the other two pieces of bread on top of the cheese. Brush the top and bottom of the sandwiches with olive oil.
- Cook the Panini on medium heat for 4 to 6 minutes, flipping halfway through. The bread should be toasted, and the cheese should be melted.

Goat Cheese Pesto and Egg English Muffin Panini

This Panini features some lovely contrasting flavors. The goat cheese has a strong flavor that's tempered by the aromatic flavor of the peso, and the rich flavor of the eggs. If you're not a fan of goat cheese try using half as much goat cheese or no goat cheese at all! It's truly a treat anyway you decide to make it!

Prep Time: 20 Minutes
Cook Time: 5 Minutes
Servings: 4

INGREDIENTS

4 egg
4 English muffins, split and lightly toasted
4 tablespoons prepared pesto
4 oz. Humboldt Fog goat cheese or Bucheron de chevre, sliced into 4 rounds
4 large tomato slices
8 leaves radicchio
Olive oil
4 teaspoon butter

DIRECTIONS

› Use a whisk to beat the eggs with a pinch of salt and pepper. Place the butter in a skillet and melt it on medium heat. Use a spoon to stir the eggs and push them across the pan. Cook until the eggs set, about 1 to 2 minutes.
› Spread the pesto on the inside of part of the English muffins, then layer the eggs on the inside of the lower piece of the English muffin, then the cheese, then the radicchio, then the tomatoes, and top with the other half of the English muffin. Brush the top and bottom of the sandwiches with olive oil.
› Cook the Panini on medium heat for 4 to 5 minutes, flipping halfway through. The English muffin should be toasted, and the cheese should be melted.

NEXT ON THE LIST!

Here's What You Do Now...

If you were please with our book then please leave us a review on amazon where you purchased this book! In the world of an author who writes books independently, your reviews are not only touching but important so that we know you like the material we have prepared for "you" our audience! So leave us a review...we would love to see that you enjoyed our book!

If for any reason that you were less than happy with your experience then send me an email at **Feedback@Healthylifestylerecipes.org** and let me know how we can better your experience. We always come out with a few volumes of our books and will possibly be able to address some of your concerns. Do keep in mind that we strive to do our best to give you the highest quality of what "we the independent authors" pour our heart and tears into.

I am very happy to create new and exciting recipes and do appreciate your purchase. I thank you for your many great reviews and comments! With a warm heart! ~Katherine Archer "Professional Loving Chef" ...Xoxo ;)

ABOUT THE AUTHOR

Katherine Archer is a Professional Gourmet Chef that has over 15 years experience with her craft traveling the world perfecting her craft. These special recipes within this book are some of her own personal favorites that have also been a specialty in the homes of many famous celebrities. Her profession calls for her to visit many well known names to cater special events and whip up some of the best Panini's she can offer. In her spare time she enjoys perfecting her craft, walks on the beach. She mostly enjoys putting together books to share her delicious recipes with you!

FREE BOOKS!!

New Books, Pro Cooking Tips, & Recipes Sent to Your Email

For our current readers...if you like receiving free books, pro cooking tips & recipes to add to your collection, then this is for you! This is for promoting our material to our current members so you can review our new books and give us feed back when we launch new books we are publishing! This helps us determine how we can make our books better for you, our audience! Just go to the url below and leave your name and email. We will send you a complimentary book about once a month.

Get My Free Book

Healthylifestylerecipes.org/Freebook2review

OTHER MUST HAVE RECIPE BOOKS!

Crisper Basket Recipe Cookbook is one of our favorite stories yet! You will love and enjoy all of these mouth watering ways to crisp up that food without using grease or oils because you make meals in your very own oven. Air Fryer style cooking recipes right in the comfort of your own home! Great gift for anyone to enjoy!
https://www.amazon.com/Crisper-Basket-Recipe-Cookbook-Multi-Purpose/dp/1974510565

If you are looking for amazing foods that go great for any occasion then you should check out **"Ceramic Titanium Cookbook"** by Sasha Hassler & Allison August! There are many delicious foods and desserts that can be made in this non-stick ceramic titanium fry pan. With over 99 different recipes you will become a large fan of this great Amazon selling cookbook! Click the link below to get yours!
http://www.amazon.com/Ceramic-Titanium-Cookbook-Delicious-Nutritious/dp/1545047995

Sandwich Recipe Notes:

Sandwich Recipe Notes:

18478580R00047

Printed in Great Britain
by Amazon